# Alice
## Out of the Box

A collection of Wonderland-themed dolls

Alison Boyd Rasmussen

Copyright © 2012 by Alison Boyd Rasmussen
Published by The Fashion Doll Review
PO Box 19851
San Diego, CA 92159-0851

All rights reserved. No part of this book may be reproduced in any form without written permission from the author except in the case of brief quotations in critical articles and reviews.

The author is not affiliated with any doll company. The photos and opinions expressed in this book do not reflect the opinions of any companies.

Tonner®, Tyler Wentworth® and Antoinette® are registered trademarks of Tonner Doll Company. Fashion Royalty®, The Dynamite Girls®, and Nu. Face® are registered trademarks of Integrity Toys. Barbie® and Liddle Kiddles® are a registered trademarks of Mattel. Alex® is a registered trademark of Alexander Doll Company. Moxie Girlz® is a registered trademark of MGA Entertainment.

For more information, contact the editor of The Fashion Doll Review at alison@fashiondollreview.com or www.fashiondollreview.com.

ISBN: 0983681627
ISBN-13: 978-0983681625

## Dedication

This book is dedicated to the loyal readers of the Fashion Doll Review, those who followed the Alice Project, Alice in Wonderland fans, and my wonderful family.

Soft plush Alice, created from vintage, recycled fabrics for the *Go Ask Alice* show in Santa Barbara in 2009 by Cimmerii.

OPPOSITE: Boots from Tonner Doll Company's Alice Kingsleigh.

## Why Alice?

Any girl who wanders around drinking strange bottles labeled, "Drink Me," and eating cake all day has what it takes to make it in today's hectic world. No other hero has quite the same mixture of befuddlement, bemusement, and creativity. On a personal level, I can relate to her--in more ways than I care to admit.

Combining Alice with the wonderful world of dolls creates a delightful union: a handheld work of art to rework, restyle, display, and photograph, with roots in literature and with which to be inspired. Within these pages, I hope to motivate you to create your own imaginative collection.

Additionally, where might *I* find Alice's potions, cakes, and mushrooms, so that I might grow or shrink to fit my current lifestyle? If I discovered such a product, think of the profit that might be made.

## How to use this book

This book's sole purpose is eye candy. It's frivolous fandom, and I've created it to feature some favorite dolls for you and for my dear blog readers. Hopefully I will open your mind to a new hobby--if you aren't already a doll collector, or you haven't photographed your own collection. I've provided a list of resources in the back of the book to help you find the featured dolls and artists.

Please keep in mind I'm not a professional photographer--I do this as a hobby, and my style might feel a little grungy to you. Feel free to direct any questions or comments to my blog, the Fashion Doll Review: www.fashiondollreview.com. You can also email me at alison@fashiondollreview.com.

I hope you enjoy this book as much as I have creating it!

# Alice: Vinyl and Plastic
## Tonner

The Tonner Doll Company makes gorgeous dolls in all sizes. Some are designed as Alice, but the two on these pages have been restyled to fit my own interpretation.

La Belle Grande American Model stands 22" tall. Mod Alice in her one-of-a-kind halter dress by Nancie of Nankatts Designs, I adore her smokey eyes and applied lashes.

OPPOSITE: Marvelously Morose Sister Dreary is a 16" tall vinyl beauty with magenta eyes and was a Tonner Halloween convention exclusive. Her dress is the same style as La Belle Grande's and also by Nankatts. She wears her original hat and choker.

Re-Imagination Alyce uses Tonner's Stella sculpt. She is one of my favorite out-of-the-box Alice dolls available on the market.

Her pensive expression gives her a sad and thoughtful look. Check out the amazing lace trim and hoop skirt on her chiffon dress!

From Tim Burton's Alice in Wonderland collection, Tonner Doll Company acquired the license to produce some amazing dolls and outfits from this movie.

Alice Kingsleigh's sculpt is based on the likeness of actor Mia Wasikowska.

Tea Party Crasher is a scaled down version of the Mia Wasikowska head on the 10" Tiny Kitty body, dressed in the Mad Hatter's teapot dress.

This outfit includes a bandage for Alice's arm--an interesting little detail.

Growing bigger and bigger, Um from Umbridge appears on the 22" American Model body. She is dressed in a black, white, and red fashion from the Red Queen's court.

NEXT TWO PAGES:
LEFT: Cherished Friends exclusive Through the Looking Glass Alice on the 12" Marley body from my friend Carolyn Mitrovich's collection.

RIGHT: Blue Alice Halloween convention exclusive from 2011. She features the Shauna head sculpt on the Antoinette body.

From the Cinderella collection, Euphemia has been restyled as a brunette Alice, dressed in Alice Kingsleigh's outfit.

I've restyled the Ghost of Christmas Past (Daphne) as a steampunk version of Alice, using the gloves from her original outfit, Alyce's dress, the corset from Lilah's outfit (Jonah Hex collection), and an oversized hat by DollHeart.

## Integrity Toys

These 12" glittering divas make lovely grown-up Alice dolls. They appear more confident and less befuddled than traditional Alice.

Misaki (FR Nippon On The Go Destination: Tokyo) has been dressed in Dynamite Girls Jolly Jett's fashion, ribbon, tulle, and Momoko boots.

W Club exclusive Bewitching Hour Luchia Z projects nothing but confidence with cocktail in hand, wearing a pale blue sparkling dress by Mattel.

Drink me? I think I will!

The companion doll from International Fashion Doll Convention 2010, Curiouser, was a must-have for my Alice collection. Her fun Lolita-style look brings a little bang to the cabinet.

The souvenir doll from 2010 IFDC did not disappoint: The Red Queen uses the Tatyana head sculpt in a couture style gown. She's ravishing in red.

I Love How You Love Me Poppy Parker makes an appearance as Alice as well, with her sweet face and wholesome look.

This wholesome look is somewhat counteracted by her Lolita-style outfit, borrowed from Curiouser, the IFDC convention companion doll.

## Mattel

PREVIOUS PAGES:

Left: Alice in Wonderland by Mattel, rebodied on a Nu.Face body by Integrity Toys. Displayed with Momoko, Aria (Dynamite Girl) in Mattel, Poppy Parker Beatnik Blues, and Misaki (Integrity Toys).

Right: Vintage Storybook Liddle Kiddle Alice Wonderliddle, 1968 by Mattel.

## Alexander Doll Company

Alice a la Gwen Stefani, as imagined by Carol Peters, talented doll artist. Alex (Alexander Doll Company) models this fashion, which includes tights, a tiered skirt, vest, bodice, jewelry, and pocket watch.

Lala Pullip by Jun Planning (now manufactured by Groove) is a 2009 San Diego Comic Con exclusive. She is modeling a one-of-a-kind outfit by MegannArt.

You can see details of the handmade bunny opposite.

Sweet Poodle Momoko is a one-of-a-kind doll created for IFDC and donated by PetWorks for the raffle. She is modeling Modern Alice, also created by MegannArt. She projects a sophisticated, stylish Alice.

## Other Vinyl

Takara Jenny created this Birthday Club Jenny doll in 2005. Yes, she is wearing a crown--but who says Alice can't be queen in her own right?

OPPOSITE: Moxie Girl Avery makes an appearance as Alice.

## Resin Alice
### Berdine Creedy

Berdine Creedy ball-jointed dolls are known for their sweet faces and large, often pouty lips.

Butterfly Child Harmoni is wearing Dressed Up Alice, designed by Paulette Goodreau for Creedy's collection. She is shown with Mod Alice, also on the opposite page, who has been redressed in assorted Michele Hardy pieces.

OPPOSITE: Mod Alice uses the Uniti face sculpt, and is one of just 10 dolls created exclusively for the store Wishes and Dreams. Her face-up, outfit, and wig are created by Michele Hardy.

# Goodreau Dolls

It's time for tea! Tiny pals Ashlyn (5") and Adeline Joy (8") are dressed for the occasion. Adeline Joy is wearing an outfit designed for Goodreau's Snappy dolls and a wig by Michele Hardy.

OPPOSITE: 16" Whisper has outgrown her cage in Goodreau's Come Home Alice outfit.

Whisper, also our cover model, shows off an edgy denim Alice design by Jennygrey. This outfit includes a strapless zip-up dress, lace-edged tulle apron, gloves, ballet slippers, hat, and pocket watch.

Innuendo takes a turn modeling a one-of-a-kind outfit created by Michele Hardy. This dress includes a printed dress, apron, sleeves, bloomers, stockings, and charm necklace.

Whisper has had a makeover!

Her new look is provided by Beesou of Overnight Flight.

I've added a little bling to the Come Home Alice outfit as well.

# Kim Lasher BJDs

Ever expressive, Kim's ball-jointed beauties provide collectors with something extra special. While Kim has created dolls specifically with an Alice theme, Anya, featured here, has been restyled to look like Alice.

Anya wears a raven wig by Peak's Woods and an Effanbee Flexi-pose outfit from the Curiouser and Curiouser vinyl doll. The pastel blue highlights her soft glass eyes.

In a cropped Kemper wig and edgy denim outfit by Jennygrey, Anya takes on more modern look.

Simply Alice is a gorgeous 23" tall beauty created by Kim Lasher to reflect another Alice interpretation. Puzzled or sad? You decide.

Alice is wearing a blonde wig by Luts.

OPPOSITE: In a red Monique wig and outfit by Michele Hardy, Alice takes on a more whimsical look.

# Tiny Asian BJD Alice

Full set JiaJia as Alice is a limited edition ball-jointed doll of just 10 dolls, created by Doll-Leaves.

Besides her unique, surprised open mouth, she has a fully posable body (16 cm) and a full blonde wig. Her fun dress includes a tulle apron, and she has stockings, shoes, and a hair bow as well.

Bayer, a LaTi Yellow, is a Korean BJD and is about same size as JiaJia. Her outfit is crafted of silk and satin, lace with ribbon roses, and includes lace panties, too.

She was a limited edition from December 2011.

Mini Gem Uyoo is a 29 cm (about 11.5") girl by Soom. She is dressed in Takara Jenny's costume.

Elfdoll Olivia is a 16 cm (5.5") tall BJD who has been restyled in a ribbon and lace Alice costume.

Olivia and Uyoo share a secret: they are the only two girls with elf ears in this book.

## Medium and Large ABJDs

Peak's Woods, from Korea, makes my favorite ball-jointed dolls. I own one of almost every sculpt.

Sky, shown here and opposite, was my first Peak's Woods girl. Here, she appears ethereal as a shepherd Alice, in a Tibetan lambswool wig by Michele Hardy.

OPPOSITE: She is a little edgier as Dark Alice, in Nankatts halter top dress.

Often, when playing in the world of the ball-jointed doll, Alice becomes a little softer.

Melin by Dollzone rests soundly in her lovely full set outfit. It includes pink hose and platform shoes, a lace skirt, chiffon floral leggings, crocheted floral dress with sequined ties, a neck ruff, and a hair bow.

OPPOSITE: Peak's Woods Wake-Up Lottie (hybrid on a Fairy of Bugs body) is having a go in the same outfit. Though she doesn't look thrilled, she simply sparkles in it!

Resinsoul Lan from China (a slim MSD) stands about 16" tall and can share clothes with Tyler Wentworth. She is modeling Alyce's outfit. She has had a face-up by Leah Lilly of Froggy Duds.

DollHeart has created some wonderful Alice-inspired fashions over the years.

One of the most coveted is Alice Fantasy, as modeled by Sky.

It includes detachable sleeves (with buttons) and an apron, so you can change the look.

Whether you prefer whimsical, classic or modern Alice looks, you're bound to find something you love in the ball-jointed doll world. If you can't find exactly what you want, you can commission it!

Peak's Woods Skiya is sharing a sweet moment with her friend flamingo.

Her wig by DollHeart. Skiya's one-of-a-kind outfit was designed and created by Carol Peters and is called Rococo Alice.

Dollzone Morphoa has had a Leah Lilly makeover. She is modeling DollHeart's Alice Underground outfit with a hat by Jennygrey.

Peak's Woods Goldie wears Tweedle Dee from Val Zeitler's exclusive DollHeart collection, offered by *Haute Doll* magazine.

Wake-Up Cue, also by Peak's Woods, is shown here in Alice Fantasy by DollHeart, wig by Michele Hardy, and hat by Tonner Doll Company.

Yeru the Soul (Peak's Woods) is shown here on a shorter Fairy of Bugs body, and is displayed with Kim Lasher's Anya. Yeru is dressed in a one-of-a-kind outfit by Michele Hardy, and Anya is dressed in Jennygrey.

OPPOSITE: Lady Alice by Peak's Woods is a tiny size ball-jointed doll. Her outfit was a limited edition full-set offered by the company in the fall on 2011. Lady Alice also appears on the back cover of the book.

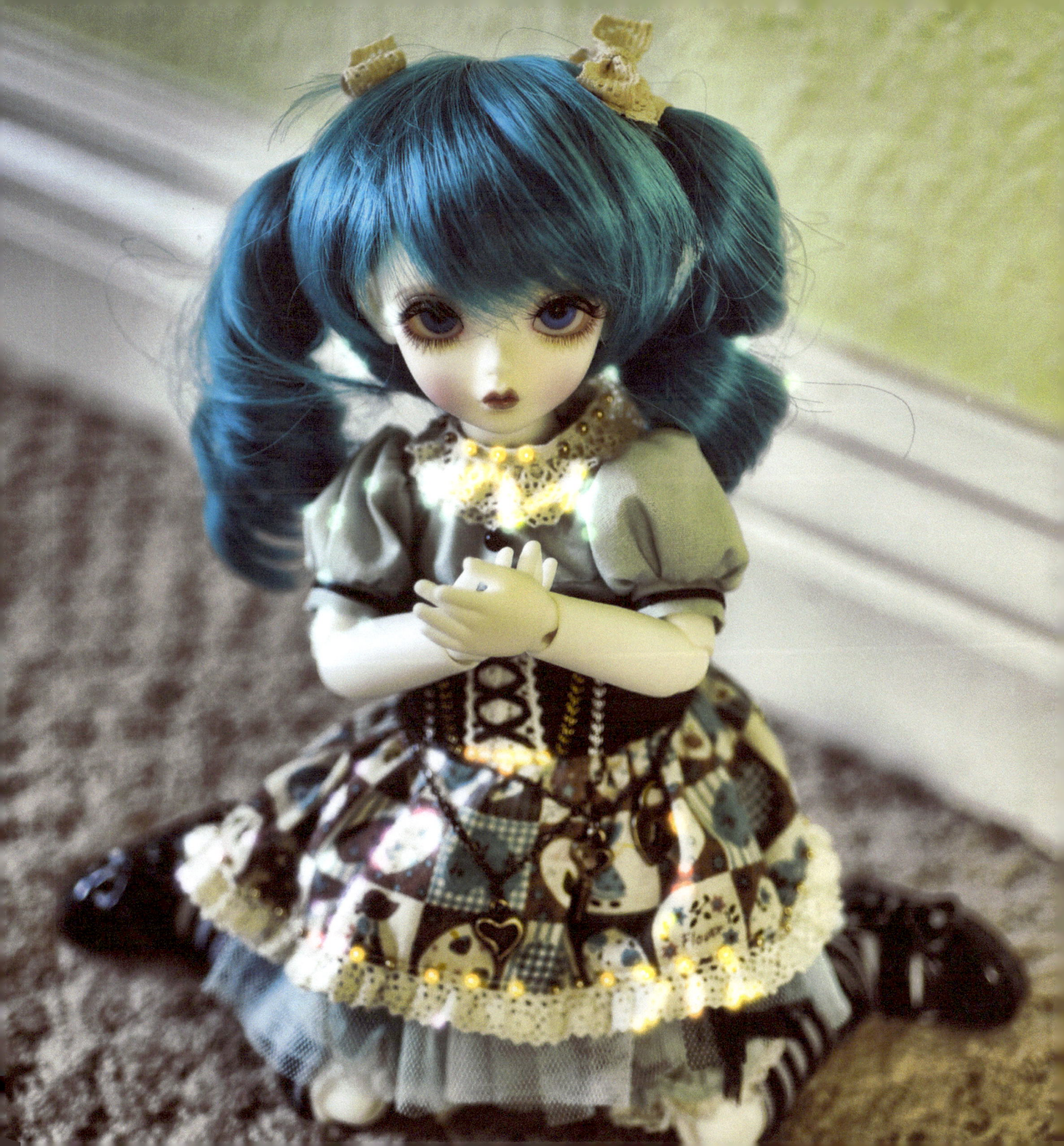

Morphoa by Dollzone makes another appearance in Queen of Hearts by DollHeart.

Her wig is also by DollHeart, and her red glass eyes are original.

Tan Briana by Peak's Woods is an exclusive from The Glamour collection. She is dressed in Pink Alice by DollHeart.

NEXT PAGE:
Peak's Woods Lottie in Tweedle Dee by Val Zeitler.

Briana (white skin version) with a face-up by Beesou of Overnight Flight in Val Zeitler's Tight Rope Walker outfit.

This fun little hybrid uses Dollmore's Lukia Sky head and a Peak's Woods Fairy of Fairytales body.

She is dressed in Little Pinky Alice by DollHeart, which includes the shoes.

Peak's Woods Sky with a new face-up by Leah Lilly of Froggy Duds, dressed in Val Zeitler's Tweedle Dee.

Limhwa Mimi in DollHeart Little Pinky Alice and Leekeworld mohair wig.

OPPOSITE: Tan Briana by Peak's Woods in Val Zeitler's Drink Me outfit.

# Resources

These are links to the dolls modeling in this book.

| | |
|---|---|
| Alexander Doll Company | http://www.madamealexander.com |
| Berdine Creedy | http://www.berdinecreedy.com |
| Doll Leaves | http://www.doll-leaves.com |
| Doll-Zone | http://www.doll-zone.com |
| Dollmore | http://www.dollmore.net |
| Elfdoll | http://elfdollshop.com/index.php |
| Goodreau Dolls | http://www.goodreaudoll.com |
| Integrity Toys | https://www.integritytoys.com |
| Kim Lasher | http://www.lasherbjds.com |
| LaTi BJDs | http://www.latidoll.com |
| Limhwa BJDs | http://www.flickr.com/photos/eosdoll |
| Mattel | http://www.mattel.com |
| Momoko | http://www.momokodoll.com/en/ |
| Moxie Girlz | http://www.moxiegirlz.com |
| Peak's Woods | http://www.peakswoods.net |
| Pullip | http://www.groove.ws |
| Resin Soul | http://www.resinsoul.com |
| Soom | http://www.dollsoom.com/soom/ |
| Takara Tomy | http://www.takaratomy.co.jp/english/index.html |
| Tonner Doll Company | http://www.tonnerdoll.com |

Additionally, you will find the following artists and manufacturers in my photos:

| | |
|---|---|
| Carol Peters | http://www.fashiondollreview.com |
| Cimmerii | http://thedollhead.blogspot.com |
| DollHeart | http://www.dollheart.com |
| Effanbee | http://www.effanbeedoll.com |
| Jennygrey | http://jennygrey.etsy.com |
| Leah Lilly and Froggy Duds | http://www.froggyduds.com |
| Megann Art | http://www.megannart.com |
| Michele Hardy | http://www.michelehardy.com/BJD.html |
| Nankatts | http://nankatts.etsy.com |
| Overnight Flight | http://www.denofangels.com/forums/showthread.php?377690 |
| Val Zeitler | http://site.valsdolldesigns.com |

Thanks for giving me permission to feature your wonderful dolls and outfits in this book. Carolyn, thanks for letting me sneak a photo of your gorgeous girl in here, too.

I am not affiliated with these doll companies or the clothing manufacturers. I'm a fan who thinks you should support these artists with your wallets. Thank you!.

You can find me at my blog, The Fashion Doll Review: http://www.fashiondollreview.com, where I am happy to receive your comments.

www.ingramcontent.com/pod-product-compliance
Lightning Source LLC
Chambersburg PA
CBHW061357090426
42743CB00002B/44